Rabbits

Contents

Wild rabbits   page 2

Rabbit ears   page 4

Rabbit noses   page 6

Rabbit legs   page 8

Kinds of pet rabbit   page 10

A home for your pet   page 12

Looking after rabbits   page 14

Glossary   page 16

Written by
Vicky Shipton

Wild rabbits

burrow

In the wild, rabbits live with other rabbits.

Rabbits dig burrows, so the claws on their front paws are sharp.

Rabbit ears

Each ear can turn in a different direction.

With their long ears, rabbits can pay attention to every sound.

Predators hunt rabbits for food.

If a rabbit hears something coming, it gets ready to run away.

Rabbit noses

Rabbits twitch their noses to pick up smells, especially from predators.

Sometimes rabbits twitch their noses quickly. This is the first signal that they may be scared.

Rabbit legs

A rabbit's back legs are long and strong. They help it to change direction if it is being chased.

foot thumping the ground

If a rabbit thinks something is coming,
it may thump its back foot on the ground.

Kinds of pet rabbit

A **lop-eared rabbit** has really long ears.

Rabbits make wonderful, loving pets. There are lots of different kinds of rabbits.

The biggest kind of rabbit is called the Flemish Giant. These gentle rabbits are quite heavy. They can weigh up to nine kilos!

A home for your pet

mesh front for protection

Most owners keep their pet rabbit in an outside **hutch** like this.

Other owners prefer to keep their pet rabbits inside. It is fun to watch them play!

Looking after rabbits

Leaves and vegetables are the best food for rabbits.

To stay healthy, a rabbit needs fresh food and water every day.

Always be gentle with rabbits. Check they are in a comfortable position when you pick them up.

Glossary

burrow a big hole that wild rabbits dig

hutch an outdoor home for a pet rabbit

lop-eared rabbit a kind of rabbit with floppy ears

predators animals that eat other animals